Going to the Market

by Jeanne Tao

Illustrated by Jaime Zollars

Glenview, Illinois • Boston, Massachusetts • Chandler, Arizona
Upper Saddle River, New Jersey

Mama made a list of errands. She asked, "Lisa, can you go out for me?"
"Can I go too?" asked Jenny.
"What can you do?" Lisa asked Jenny.
"I can help carry things," she said.
"OK," said Mama. "Be careful."

"This is a long list," said Lisa. "We have many places to go."

"Where will we go first?" asked Jenny.

"To buy curry," said Lisa.

"What is curry?" asked Jenny.

"Curry is a spice, something that gives flavor to food, like salt or pepper," said Lisa. "Mama uses curry when she cooks."

curry

They went to the store together.

"Good morning, girls," said Mr. Sharma. "How can I help you?"

"We need some curry for dinner tonight," said Lisa.

"You came to the right place," said Mr. Sharma. He gave them a box of curry powder.

Lisa paid Mr. Sharma for the curry powder. Then the girls said good-bye.

---

powder: something that is in very small pieces, almost like dust

"What else do we have to buy? What is next on the list?" asked Jenny.

"We need tomatoes," said Lisa. "I know where to go to buy them. Mrs. Rios has a vegetable stand at the outdoor market."

"What is a stand? And what is a market?" asked Jenny.

"A stand is a place to buy things," answered Lisa. "And a market is place to sell things. You can buy vegetables at a vegetable stand. Some people sell vegetables outside, in outdoor markets."

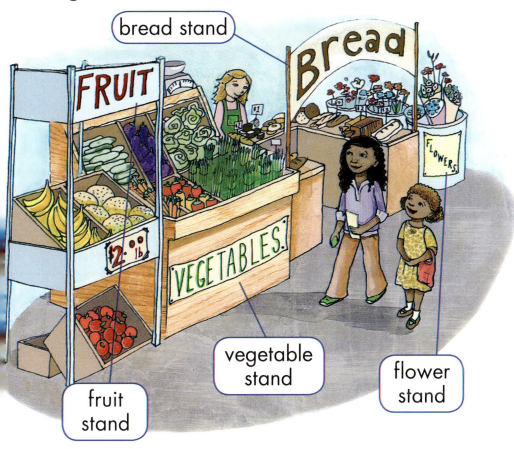

"How can I help you, girls?" asked Mrs. Rios.

"We need some tomatoes, for dinner" said Lisa.

"I have beautiful tomatoes for you," said Mrs. Rios.

The girls bought three beautiful tomatoes. Mrs. Rios put the tomatoes in a bag. She gave the bag to Lisa. Lisa gave the bag to Jenny.

"What is next on the list? What else do we have to buy?" asked Jenny.

"We need fish," said Lisa. "Mr. Li sells fish in this market. We always buy fish from Mr. Li."

"I like to eat fish. Will we eat fish with curry and tomatoes?" asked Jenny.

"You'll see," said Lisa. Would you like to carry the fish too?"

fish stand

"Hello, Lisa. Hello, Jenny," said Mr. Li. "What can I do for you today?"

"We want that big fish, right there," said Lisa.

Mr. Li wrapped the big fish in a piece of paper. Lisa paid for it. She gave the fish to Jenny to carry home.

"What else do we have to buy? What is next on the list?" asked Jenny.

"We need parsley for dinner," said Lisa, "but I can't remember what parsley is."

"I know," said Jenny. "It is a small, green plant with curly leaves. I didn't see any parsley on the shelves in the market today."

On their way home, the girls saw their neighbor, Mrs. Jones.

"I see that you girls went shopping for your mother?" she asked.

"Yes," said Jenny, "but we couldn't find any parsley."

"Parsley?" said Mrs. Jones, "I grow parsley in my garden."

parsley

"This is parsley," said Mrs. Jones. "I'll cut some for you."

"Thank you so much, Mrs. Jones!" said Lisa.

"You're welcome, Lisa," said Mrs. Jones. "But, look! Jenny has all of the bags. Can you help her?"

"Oh, of course!" said Lisa. "I'm sorry, Jenny. Give me two of those bags to carry home."

The girls walked home together.

"Did you get everything we need for dinner?" asked Mama.

"Yes," said Lisa. " We got curry powder from Mr. Sharma. We got tomatoes from Mrs. Rios. We got fish from Mr. Li, and we got parsley from Mrs. Jones."

"Did you help carry the bags, Jenny?" asked Mama.

"Yes!" said Jenny. "In fact, I carried ALL of the bags home."